IMAGES
of America

BELCHERTOWN

Doris M. Dickinson and Cliff McCarthy

ISBN 978-1-5316-6020-8

Published by Arcadia Publishing
Charleston, South Carolina

For all general information contact Arcadia Publishing at:
Telephone 843-853-2070
Fax 843-853-0044
E-mail sales@arcadiapublishing.com
For customer service and orders:
Toll-Free 1-888-313-2665

Visit us on the Internet at www.arcadiapublishing.com

Contents

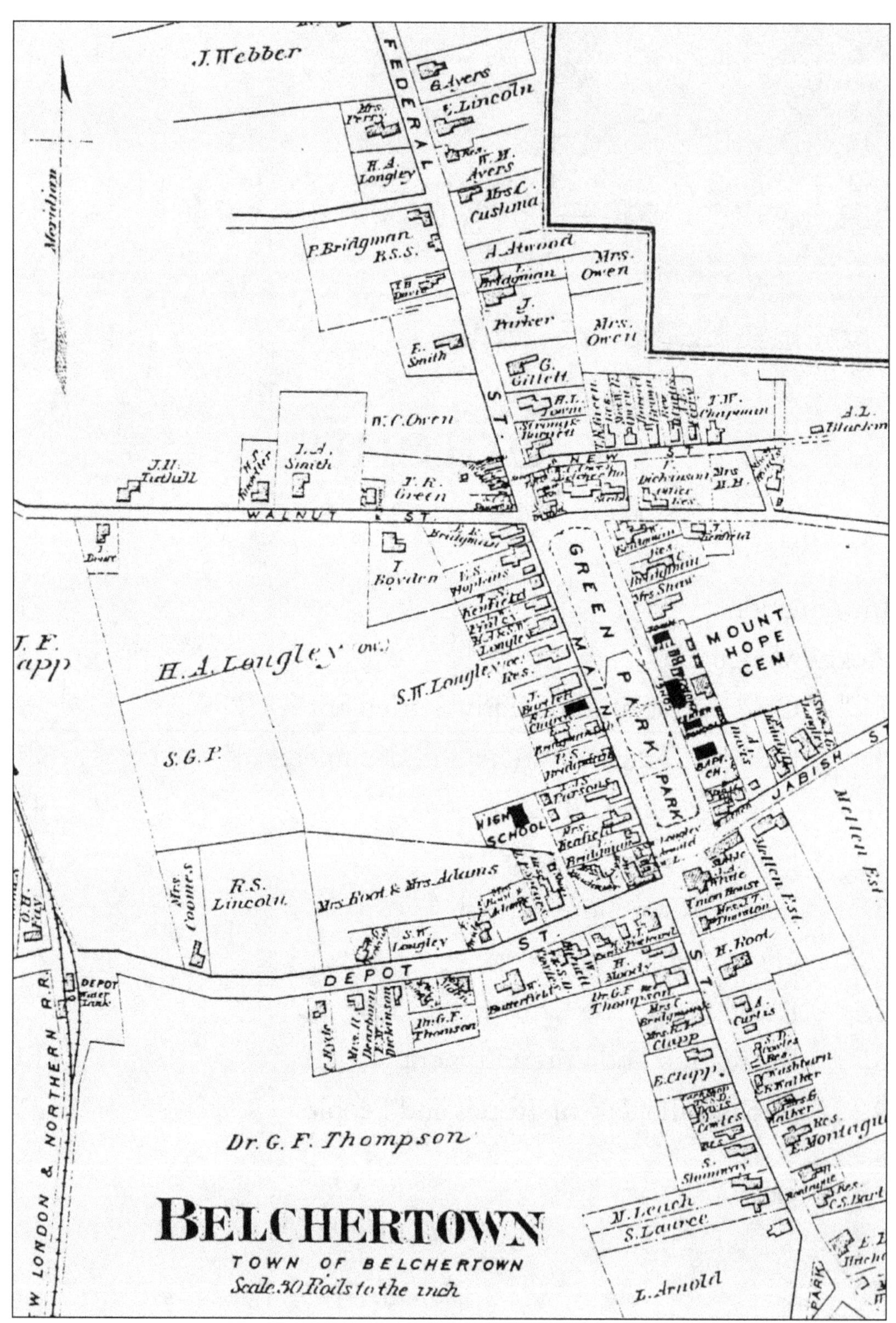

A MAP OF BELCHERTOWN CENTER, 1873.

Introduction

We hope this book is fun. Our goal in this project was to resurrect some memories, explain some mysteries, stimulate some interest, and produce a chuckle or two. It has certainly done those things for the authors, and our success will be measured by how well we have shared our fun with the reader.

We hope that some readers find in this book reasons to explore deeper into Belchertown's past and to discover the resources of the Belchertown Historical Association. Unless otherwise credited, the photographs and postcards that appear in this book are from the Association's collection at the Stone House Museum. There, many of the group photographs of people have the names listed on the back. For reasons of brevity, those names could not often be included in the captions for this book, but one can check the name of a friend or a relative by calling the Stone House or stopping by. The reader is encouraged to share his or her memories and stories.

Though this is not a comprehensive history of Belchertown, we have striven to balance some wonderful photographs with accurate explanations. In some cases, the explanations involve facts and data, while sometimes we felt a good story was in order. While trying not to perpetuate folklore as fact, we have included both and labeled each accordingly. Certainly, there are omissions that a comprehensive history could not abide. Most of these, we hope, are attributable to the limitations of the photographic material available to us.

So pull over a good reading lamp, sit back, and get comfortable with this book. In its pages, we hope newcomers and old-timers alike will discover Belchertown anew.

Acknowledgments

First and foremost, the authors would like to thank the Belchertown Historical Association for access to its archive of photographs and permission to reproduce some of these images. The wealth of information and resources to be found at the Belchertown Historical Association is astonishing. Without their cooperation, this book would not have been possible.

The authors worked with an Advisory Committee from the Belchertown Historical Association in the selection of the images and the preparation of the text. Members of this committee gave generously of their time and talents to guide and improve this work. The committee members were as follows: Shirley Bock, John Collis, Robert Hansbury, Margot Moran, James Phaneuf, and Ronald Pobieglo. All of the committee members deserve our thanks, but two gave more than asked—Shirley Bock used her amazing memory for historical detail to keep us accurate, and Margot Moran proofread and edited the text of the captions. However, as collaborative as this effort was, the authors are responsible for any mistakes or inaccuracies.

The authors would also like to thank the members of the Belchertown community who came forward and offered photographs for our use. Unfortunately, we were unable to use many that were offered and we hope that the quality of this product will justify the choices that we made. We received photographs or other material from Shirley Bock, Rachel Collard, John Collis, Agnes Hanifin, Charles Howard, Gladys Jenks, Gould Ketchen, Francis and Norman Loftus, Father Mailloux, Margot Moran, Ron Pobieglo, Ira Shattuck, Doris Stockton, and Ruthella Tucker.

The idea for this project came from respected friend Craig Della Penna, who made us believe we could do it. Daniel Lombardo, special collections curator at the Jones Library in Amherst, was also helpful and we thank him for the use of three images from the Jones Library collection. We also thank Susan Greendyke Lachevre and the Massachusetts Art Commission for use of the portrait of Governor Jonathan Belcher that hangs in the Massachusetts State House. In addition, the authors wish to thank the good people at Collective Copies in Amherst for their extra help and Jamie Carter at Arcadia Publishing for making the project as easy as possible.

Most importantly, we thank our spouses, Harvey Dickinson and Gail Gramarossa, for tolerating the frequent and numerous hours of our absence, while we pursued this project.

One

Cold Spring and the Early Settlement

COLD SPRING. The territory was first called Cold Spring for the "never failing" source of water that welcomed travelers between Hadley and Brookfield. Local legend claims that the spring was discovered by a traveler from Hatfield named Cowles and, with use, "Cowles' Spring" became "Cold Spring," the name that was applied to the area until the town's incorporation in 1761. The spring is located on the property of the University of Massachusetts Horticultural Research Center.

JONATHAN BELCHER. At its incorporation, the town was named for Jonathan Belcher, who was governor of Massachusetts and New Hampshire from 1730 to 1741. Belcher was born in Cambridge, Massachusetts, and was educated at Harvard. Although it is uncertain whether Belcher ever visited Cold Spring, he was one of the wealthy landowners who purchased a tract of the "equivalent lands" from Connecticut; lands which were then sold to settlers willing to establish a home and improve the land. Belcher also served as governor of New Jersey from 1747 until his death in 1757. He was a dedicated supporter of the College of New Jersey—later Princeton University—to which he donated his library of books. This portrait, by Frederick E. Wallace, hangs in the Massachusetts State House. The photograph was taken before significant conservation treatment was conducted on the painting. (Courtesy of Commonwealth of Massachusetts, Massachusetts Art Commission.)

STONE MILE MARKERS. With the settlement of Brookfield to the east, a road was laid through Cold Spring connecting Brookfield to Northampton and Hadley. This road became known locally as the "Bay Road." In Belchertown, three stones mark distances on this ancient route. The three existing stones are located at the corner of Route 9 and George Hannum Road, by Lawrence Memorial Hall, and at South Cemetery on Route 181.

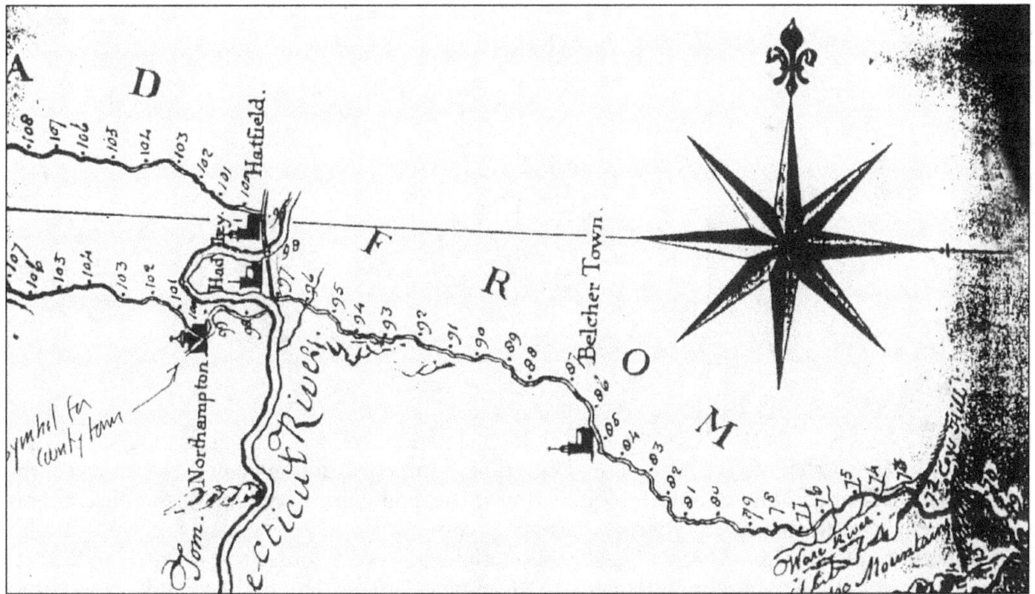

A PORTION OF A MAP, C. 1760S. Some say the markers were placed between 1765 and 1782 as a secondary route of the post road system established by colonial postmaster Benjamin Franklin for tracking the distances each piece of mail traveled. Others suggest an earlier date, citing maps like this one showing the Bay Road through Belcher's Town with the locations of the markers. (Courtesy of Special Collections and Archives, W.E.B. DuBois Library, University of Massachusetts, Amherst.)

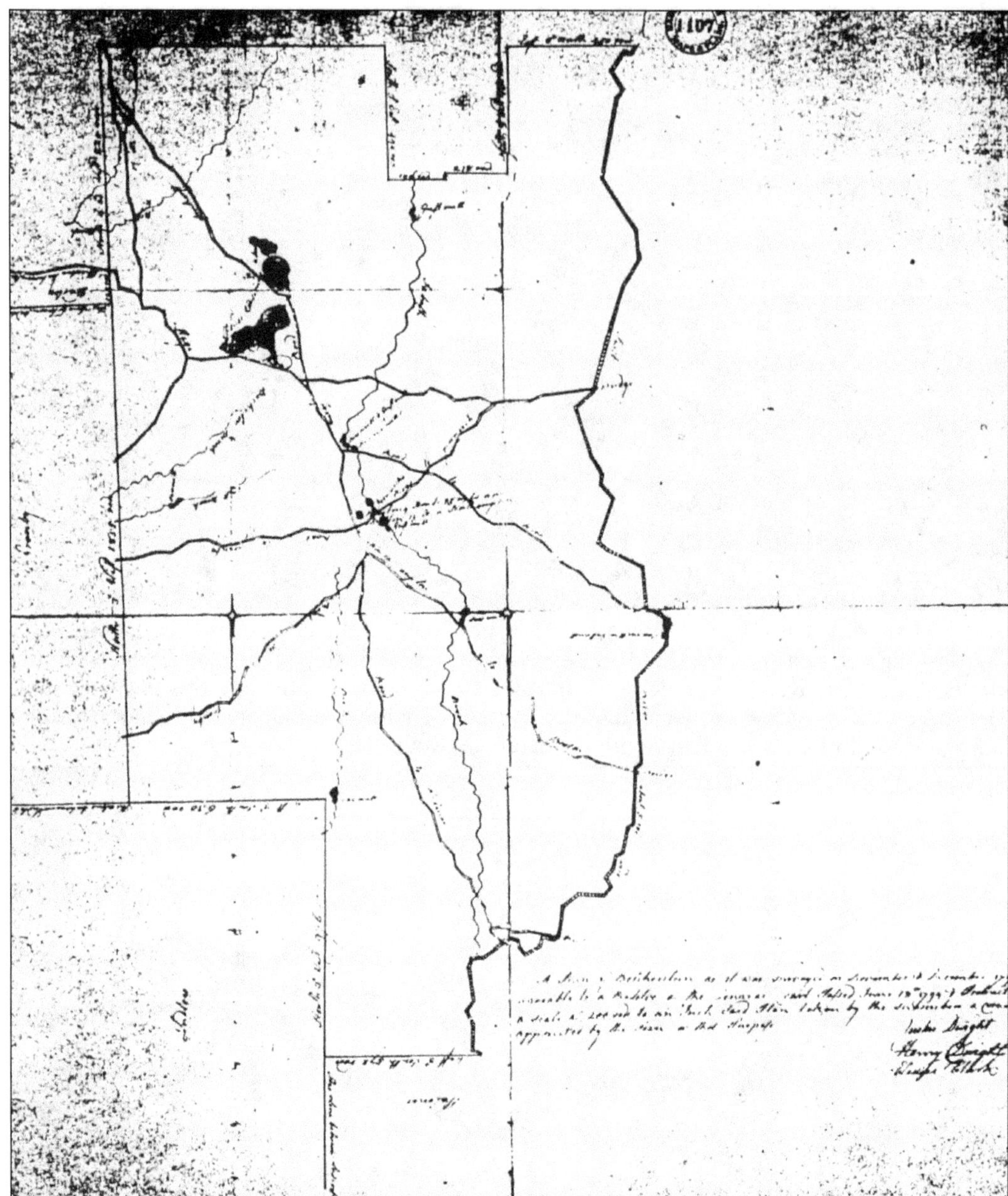

A MAP OF BELCHERTOWN, 1795. The land that comprises present-day Belchertown was once part of Connecticut. In early colonial times, the boundary between Massachusetts and Connecticut was disputed and when the area was re-surveyed, the towns of Somers, Enfield, Woodstock, and Suffield—which Massachusetts claimed—were found to be in Connecticut. In exchange for them, Massachusetts ceded to Connecticut the "equivalent lands," including what would become Belchertown, Pelham, and parts of Ware. In 1716, Connecticut sold the equivalent lands to 16 men from Massachusetts and Connecticut, and the area eventually came back under Massachusetts's jurisdiction. The proceeds from sales of the equivalent lands were used for the endowment of Yale College. This is a portion of an early map that was made by Justus Dwight and others when they surveyed the land for the General Court.

JUSTUS AND SARAH DWIGHT. The Dwight family was instrumental in the town's development. Timothy Dwight first surveyed the area for the nonresident proprietors and purchased, with other men, a tract of 1,200 acres. In 1732, Timothy's brother Nathaniel settled in Cold Spring and over time purchased hundreds of acres, including all of what is now South Main Street and the center of town. Nathaniel, who married Hannah Lyman, was prominent in the civil and religious affairs of the town, serving as the first town clerk and as a selectman. He also was a captain during the French and Indian War and active in the American Revolution. Justus, born in 1739, was a surveyor like his father and grandfather before him. He also was a selectman and represented Belchertown on the General Court and at the Massachusetts convention to ratify the U.S. Constitution. He voted "nay." His wife was Sarah Lamb Dwight.

Church Building on the Common. The building shown here, erected on land donated by Elijah Dwight in the center of town, replaced a more rudimentary meetinghouse in 1792. The original meetinghouse in Cold Spring, established by 20 families in about 1738, was located on present-day South Main Street. Prior to the separation of church and state, it took an act of town meeting to appropriate funds for meetinghouse repairs.

Warner's Tavern. Beginning in 1799, Elisha Warner owned a tavern in this building, now 50 Federal Street. According to tradition, the tavern was a stop on the stagecoach route from Northampton to Boston. Elisha Warner's father, Ebenezer, was an early settler and large landowner in town, arriving in 1737. Elisha, like others in his family, was active in town affairs, serving as constable, tax collector, treasurer, and town clerk. (Courtesy of Jones Library, Amherst.)

Dr. Estes Howe. The town's first physician was Estes Howe. He owned two large tracts of land on both sides of present-day North Main Street. On the westerly portion, he built a home in 1799 as a wedding present for his daughter Nancy and her husband, Ichabod Sanford, which later became known as Crystal Spring Farm. His own residence was on the easterly side of the road, with land extending south into what is presently the town common. Dr. Howe and his wife, Diana, who had previously been married to Elijah Dwight, gave this land to the town in 1803 with the provision that no permanent structures were ever to be erected upon it. A legend says that Dr. Howe, who was a surgeon during the Revolutionary War, was visited at his home by Lafayette when the general passed through Belchertown during his American tour in 1824–25.

The Town Common, 1839. This woodcut shows the town common, looking north. In the distance is the Classical School at the location of the present-day police station. The Congregational Church, in the center, originally had an entrance from the common, but had been remodeled in 1828 to provide its current entrance from the south. The Brainerd Church building, now St. Francis Church, is shown next to it.

Two

Industry, Transportation, and Commerce

A Main Street Panorama. This panoramic photograph of the center of town was taken from atop Lawrence Memorial Hall shortly after it was built in 1923.

The Tertius and Samuel Cowles Carriage Manufactory. In the nineteenth century, Belchertown was a center for the production of carriages, buggies, and sleighs. Belchertown carriage makers such as Packard, Chandler & Hitchcock, H.T. Filer, Maynard Leach, Wright & Pepper, and the Cowles' company (pictured here) sent carriages to places as far away as England, Australia, and Persia. Long convoys of carriages were taken south to Virginia, Georgia, Alabama, and Mississippi for use on plantations.

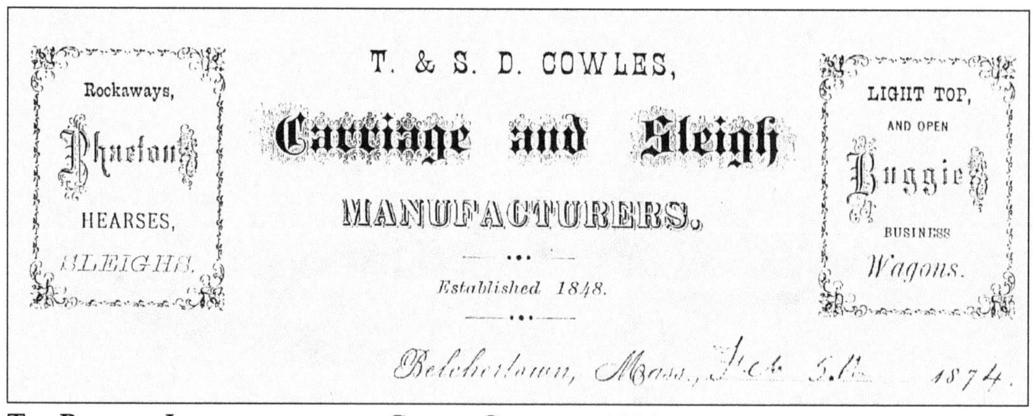

Rockaways,
Phaetons,
HEARSES,
SLEIGHS.

T. & S. D. COWLES,
Carriage and Sleigh
MANUFACTURERS.
Established 1848.

LIGHT TOP,
AND OPEN
Buggies
BUSINESS
Wagons.

Belchertown, Mass., Feb. 5th 1874.

The Business Letterhead of the Cowles Company, 1874.

TERTIUS COWLES. Tertius Cowles founded the T. & S.D. Cowles Carriage Manufactory with his brother, Samuel D. Cowles. The shops were located to the rear of Tertius Cowles's property on South Main Street.

EMPLOYEES OF COWLES'S CARRIAGE SHOP. In 1845, 677 wagons were made in Belchertown with a combined value of over $40,000. Ten years later, that output had increased to over $100,000.

HUMPHREY FILER. Humphrey Filer's carriage factory, one of the largest in town, was located just north of the common, on the west side of Main Street. Filer is said to have sent a very handsome buggy to Queen Victoria as a present.

CALVIN HITCHCOCK. Calvin Hitchcock ran a carriage-making business in Belchertown. In addition to local sales, he occasionally made large shipments to Chicago, which necessitated his travel to that city to oversee the delivery. In 1858, he closed his Belchertown shop and moved to Ware, where he opened a mercantile business on the corner of Church and Main Streets.

The Curtis Blacksmith Shop. Carriage making produced "spinoff" work for blacksmiths, wheelwrights, and skilled woodworkers, ironers, trimmers, and painters. Alanson Curtis, and later his son Herbert, ran one of the last blacksmith shops in Belchertown on South Main Street.

An Old Carriage Shop. Even though the carriage industry flourished in Belchertown in the 1870s, the decline really began after the Civil War, when mass production techniques began to replace the handcrafted methods used in local shops. The industry lasted to the end of the nineteenth century, when the Cowles and Leach companies were among the last to close, leaving scarcely a reminder of Belchertown's legacy as the "Detroit of the Carriage Industry." (Courtesy of Jones Library, Amherst.)

Pratt's Mill. Many mills were active in Belchertown during the heyday of the carriage industry, as the companies used mostly native ash, basswood, and oak. Farmers and loggers dragged the timbers to the mills by oxen. Virgil Pratt and his sons ran a grist, saw, and shingle mill which was built in the 1860s on Jabish Brook. The mill in this postcard view burned in August of 1900.

The Rebuilt Pratt's Mill. This photograph shows Pratt's mill as it was rebuilt. Located on Route 202 north of Route 9, it was the last working, water-powered mill on Jabish Brook when it closed in the 1950s.

THE UNION HOUSE. Situated at the nexus of several transportation routes, Belchertown was the location of a number of large hotels in the nineteenth century. This one, called the Union House or White's Tavern, was built in the eighteenth century and stood at the south end of the common until 1873. James H. Clapp bought the building in 1812 and for 20 years served passengers on his stagecoach routes. It is said that General Lafayette and Ralph Waldo Emerson dined there.

THE HIGHLAND HOTEL. Built in the 1880s, the magnificent Highland Hotel was located where the Union House stood. The building had a rooftop observatory, wide balconies, gas lighting, and steam heat. Unfortunately, the hotel burned to the ground twice, once before it even opened. It was not rebuilt after the second fire in 1892. Among the losses in the second fire was a wooden leg belonging to an employee.

THE BELCHER HOUSE. The Belcher House was located at the north end of the common, where the police station now stands, in a building that once housed the Belchertown Classical School. Promotional material of the day described the Belcher House thusly: "This is a favorite resort for the weary ones from the city, and a more restful place would be difficult to find."

THE NATIONAL ADVERTISING HOTEL REGISTER.

Maynard, Gough & Co. JOB PRINTERS, Worcester, Mass.

BELCHER HOUSE.

A. L. Burbank, Fire-Arms and Fishing Tackle, Worcester, Mass.

Drug Store!
S. B. BARNES, Proprietor.
Drugs, Medicines, AND CHEMICALS,
Fancy and Toilet Articles, Etc., Etc.
CIRCULATING LIBRARY.
CHOICE CONFECTIONERY AND CIGARS.
Lazarus & Morris' Spectacles,

Hair Dressing Rooms
Also, Billiard Room.

E. R. BRIDGMAN,
Cigar Manufacturer.
Knights Templars,
BELCHERTOWN, MASS.

BURNETT & WINTER,
Carriages and SLEIGHS,
Belchertown, Mass.

Bridgeport Spring Co.
FINK
Carriage Springs and Axles,
BRIDGEPORT, CONN.

BELCHER HOUSE
Livery Stable
First-Class Teams to Let.
J. L. BACON, Proprietor.

M. LEACH,
Carriage and Sleigh
MANUFACTURER.
All kinds of
REPAIRING
done to order.
Cor. East Main & Jabish Sts.
BELCHERTOWN, MASS.

W. E. BRIDGMAN,
DRY GOODS,
GROCERIES, PROVISIONS,
STONE WARE,
Boots, Shoes, &c.
Tobacco and Cigars.

J. R. GOULD,
Fresh and Salt MEATS,
Oysters, Lobsters,
Fish, Poultry, &c.
BELCHERTOWN, MASS.

STILES & PARKER PRESS CO.
MIDDLETOWN, CONN.
Patent Power Foot & Drop
PRESSES.

T. R. GREENE,
DRY GOODS,
Groceries, Crockery,
PROVISIONS,
GLASS & STONE WARE,
BELCHERTOWN, Mass.

C. H. SNOW,
LIGHT & HEAVY
Harnesses,
Blankets, Whips, &c.
Repairing done at Short Notice.
Davis Block, - Belchertown, Mass.

T. & S. D. COWLES,
Carriage and SLEIGH
Manufacturers,
Belchertown, Mass.
ESTABLISHED 1848.

THE STANDARD
AMERICAN BILLIARD TABLES.
H. W. COLLENDER,
No. 1 Tremont Row, Boston, Mass.

MORE THAN 8500 IN USE!
BLAKE'S
Patent Steam Pumps.
For every possible duty.
Factory, Causeway & Friend Sts., Boston.

THE BUSINESS REGISTER AT THE BELCHER HOUSE. This list of local businesses shows the importance of the carriage industry to the town. By 1898, the Belcher House had become the Park View Hotel.

The Park View Hotel. The Park View Hotel was four stories tall with broad piazzas overlooking the center of town. In addition to steam heat, the Park View had "modern plumbing and sanitation." One wing of the Park View was a facility for dancing, musicales, bowling, and billiards. The livery stable at the Park View had horses and carriages for the use of its guests.

The North End of the Common. This photograph shows the Park View Hotel and the building that now houses McCarthy's Pub. Note the pump for the well across the street from the hotel. The hotel burned in 1928.

The Belchertown Train Station. In 1853, just before the carriage industry began to fade, the trains came to Belchertown. The first tracks were built by the Palmer-Belchertown-Amherst Railroad and were leased to the New London Northern Railroad Co., later the Central Vermont Railroad (CV). Until the end of World War I, the CV operated six passenger trains daily, running from Montreal to New York City.

The Railroad Station in Belchertown. Beginning about 1891, the Central Massachusetts branch of the Boston & Maine Railroad also came through Belchertown on a separate set of tracks. Until the early 1920s, they operated 16 passenger trains daily. In the background of this photo, the old Depot Bridge can be seen. The bridge carried travelers on lower Maple Street, or Depot Street as it was called then, safely over the railroad tracks.

A Railroad Crew Shoveling Snow. In inclement weather, the steam-driven locomotives sometimes needed the assistance of human labor. During the period when both railroads used the same depot, the Belchertown stop was known as Union Station. The B & M discontinued passenger service through Belchertown in 1931 and shortly thereafter began using the Central Vermont tracks for freight service . The B & M rails were taken up in about 1943.

A Steam Engine at the Belchertown Station. The Belchertown station closed on the last day of 1961, when Romeo Joyal terminated his duties after 32 years as station agent. In the background of this photo is the Ryther & Warren company, which sold grain, coal, paint, and hardware. Ryther & Warren came to Belchertown in 1929 with the building of the Quabbin reservoir and operated until 1959, when Ryther sold the business to Grossman's hardware. The lower building eventually became the Home Fabric Mill, which closed in 1998.

THE CENTRAL VERMONT RAILROAD STATION, DWIGHT. The flag outside the station indicated that passengers were waiting to board. Trains stopped in Dwight to take on water and to pick up and deliver the mail. There was also a telegraph inside the station.

THE RAILROAD STATION, PANSY PARK. Dwight village also had a stop on the Boston & Maine line.

An Advertisement for D.D. Hazen's Ford Dealership. As the transportation industry continued to evolve, it was natural that the automobile would takes its place in Belchertown. Daniel Dwight Hazen was an acquaintance of Henry Ford, who visited Belchertown, so it followed that the first auto sales company would be a Ford dealership.

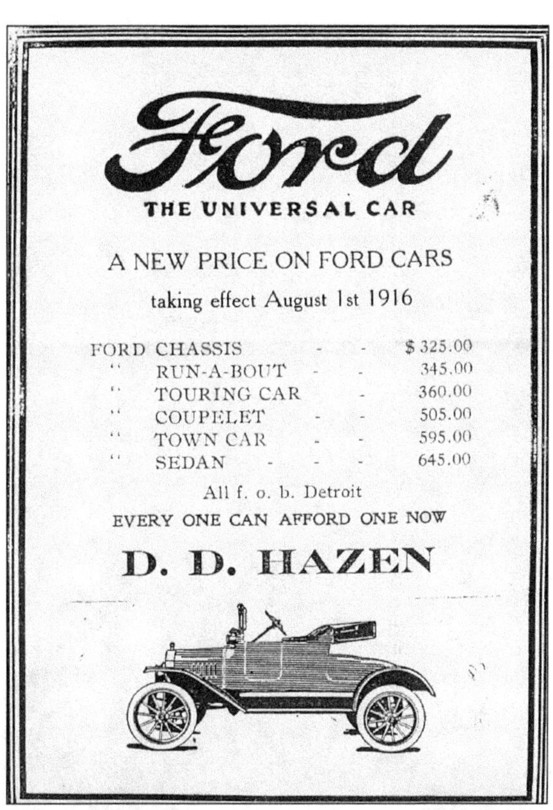

Ford

THE UNIVERSAL CAR

A NEW PRICE ON FORD CARS

taking effect August 1st 1916

FORD	CHASSIS	$ 325.00
"	RUN-A-BOUT	345.00
"	TOURING CAR	360.00
"	COUPELET	505.00
"	TOWN CAR	595.00
"	SEDAN	645.00

All f. o. b. Detroit

EVERY ONE CAN AFFORD ONE NOW

D. D. HAZEN

Belchertown Motor Sales. In 1918, D.D. Hazen opened a "demonstration building" on Jabish Street to serve his Ford Motor Company Sales Agency. The building, described as "quite citified in appearance," became a Hudson dealership in the 1940s and 1950s. It now houses a laundromat with an apartment on the second floor.

DANIEL DWIGHT HAZEN. D.D. Hazen was from one of Belchertown's leading merchant families. His father, D.L. Hazen, was proprietor of the large department store in town, and D.D. Hazen took over his father's business. D.D. Hazen was also president of the board of trade, which was instrumental in bringing the Belchertown State School to town.

A PIERCE ARROW PASSENGER BUS, C. 1919. With the rise of the automobile, a variety of new vehicles appeared to transport people around the area. This bus was used by the Belchertown Motor Coach Line run by Harold B. Ketchen. (Courtesy of Gould Ketchen.)

A SCHOOL BUS, C. 1923. The Belchertown Bus Line, owned by Harold Ketchen, brought students from Enfield and Greenwich to high school at Lawrence Memorial Hall. This bus is a 1921 Dodge that was called the "Crib" and the driver is George Ardell. (Courtesy of Gould Ketchen.)

The Holyoke, Granby, & Belchertown Express. The Holyoke, Granby & Belchertown Express was run by Harold Ketchen. It is shown here stopped in front of the Park View Hotel.

The Baggs Bus Line. M.C. Baggs operated Baggs Bus Line out of Baggs' Garage, serving Belchertown, Granby, and Holyoke.

Blue Heaven. In the 1920s, Ad Moore built the "Blue Heaven" housecar, an early recreational vehicle, for his trips to Florida. He often sent letters back to the *Sentinel*, keeping his friends abreast of his adventures. On one trip in 1928, he noted that it cost him 3¢ per mile to run the Blue Heaven and about 75¢ per day for food. He averaged about 150 miles a day.

Webster's Filling Station. The rise of the automobile brought new opportunities for business. In the 1930s, Webster's Filling Station was near the intersection of Route 9 and Bay Road, now the location of the Roadhouse Restaurant. In addition to its usual service station business, Webster's served the residents of the lakes area, selling boating equipment among its wares.

BUILDING DANIEL SHAY'S HIGHWAY. As automobiles proliferated, the demand for new roads and highways increased as well. In 1933, the construction of the Daniel Shay's Highway, or Route 202, split the Devon Lane Farm and others. The new highway was necessitated by the discontinuance of roads through the area that became the Quabbin Reservoir. (Courtesy of Ira Shattuck.)

MOVING THE SHATTUCK BARN. Building Daniel Shay's Highway required the relocation of the Shattuck barn, shown here being placed on its new foundation. (Courtesy of Ira Shattuck.)

The H.W. Conkey Home and Farm. Located on Federal Street, this was originally the Dunbar farm and then home to the Conkey family from 1923 through 1933–34, when Daniel Shay's Highway divided the property. The front portion of the building became the Village Package Store. Dunkin' Donuts and the Crossing now sit at this location.

Chadbourne's Texaco. Automobile travel gave rise to a second commercial center in Belchertown at the intersection of Routes 9 and 202. Chadbourne's Texaco was located there on the site of a station formerly owned by Paul Squires. The buildings of the old Conkey farm are in the background. The automobile changed the hospitality industry as well. In the 1950s, Smitty's Motel was across Route 202 just north of this intersection.

COOK'S MOBIL STATION, CRYSTAL SPRINGS DAIRY BAR. Prominent in this photograph are Cook's Mobil and the cows on the Crystal Springs Dairy Bar sign. The Dairy Bar was the first business in that location and was established by Andrew and Harold Ketchen. The Mobil station is now the Quabbin Service Center.

THE MAY GOLD RESTAURANT. The cows above the Crystal Springs Dairy Bar, and later the May Gold Restaurant shown here, were a well-known landmark for travelers around and through Belchertown. The big bovines met their demise in a blazing fire in 1987. Today, Hawley's Family Restaurant is located where the May Gold and the Dairy Bar once were.

Kimball & Son's. Floyd Peeso is seen sweeping the walkway in front of Kimball's appliance, radio, and television store, which was located at 5 North Main Street. The building is now the location of the Moriarty Oil Company.

Hopkins Store. Hopkins Store was built around 1850 by Samuel Hopkins and was operated by his wife, Mary, a daughter of Wright Bridgman Sr. The Hopkins family, which lived next door, ran a dry goods business on the site that is now 51 Main Street for three generations—over a century. Hopkins Store closed in 1960, and the building is presently home to Swift River Crafts.

T.R. Greene's Store. Located near where the fire station presently stands, T.R. Greene's store sold groceries and dry goods to residents at the north end of the common and to the shops across the street. Identified in this photo are, from left to right, Arthur and Eddie Richardson, Paul Shumway, Robert Chamberlain, store clerk William Burnett, Calvin Lowell, Rufus Shumway, George Gillette, and Joel Winter. An 1899 fire destroyed Greene's store.

The Brick Block, Bridgman's Store. In 1795, Wright Bridgman Sr. moved to the town center from Bay Road and opened a store on Main Street. The building in this photo, now 29 Main Street, was built about mid-century by his sons, Calvin, Phineas, and Wright Jr. The store occupied the first floor and the second story housed shops. Calvin Bridgman was a selectman, state representative, and postmaster for a number of years.

Leach's Carriage Shop and Gould's Store. The following series of photographs chronicles the evolution of the commercial buildings near the southeast corner of the common. Townspeople lined up for a photograph outside J.R. Gould's Market. A barber shop, a pharmacy, a harness shop, and Leach's Carriage Shop also occupy the block.

The Corner of Park and Jabish Streets. This photograph shows Snow's Harness Shop occupying the first floor of the building on the corner and Leach's Carriage Shop in the rear. These buildings burned in 1893.

The Gould Block. After the fire in 1893, the block was rebuilt by J.R. Gould. In this photo it was occupied by C.H. Snow's Pharmacy and H.R. Gould's Market. Henry R. Gould, son of J.R. Gould, was the proprietor.

J. RAYMOND GOULD. Ray Gould made deliveries for his father's store. He is shown here in 1905 with an unidentified companion at Croney's Corner, near the junction of Routes 21 and 202. The horse's name was Maude. Later, Ray operated the Esso service station on the corner near where his father's store once was. The gas station is now the R. & W. Service Station.

PARK STREET, THE FIRST NATIONAL STORE. Over the years, the stores have included Fuller & Dyer, a First National Store, and a Cumberland Farms. The Belchertown Pharmacy presently occupies this building. A pharmacy has been at this location since the building's construction.

Post Office Row, 1888. Main Street, near the southwest corner of the common, has been the heart of Belchertown's commercial district for a century and a half. This early scene shows Wright Bridgman's store on the corner. George Filer, a follower of health food pioneer Sylvester Graham, operated a store here in the 1840s. Note the gas streetlight on the left and the large tree in front of the store.

Post Office Row. This is Main Street, looking south. The building with the balcony, later given the address of 7 Main Street, once housed the town's first store, opened in the eighteenth century by Caleb Clark, subsequently operated by his son Eleazer, and then Samuel Foster. The store was purchased in 1837 by Henry Longley and remained in that family for many years, housing the post office for nearly a quarter-century.

Main Street. This view of the same block shows the addition of telephone poles and the absence of the streetlight on the corner. The large tree has a seat at its base, and the dark, rectangular sign beyond the tree reads, "Electricity for Light and Power, Central Mass. Electric Co." Jackson's Store was located in the third building from the corner and sold baked goods among its wares.

Hazen's Store. This postcard view shows Hazen's department store in the building which earlier had a balcony on both levels. D.L. Hazen died in 1913 and his son, Daniel Dwight Hazen, took over the business. In 1922, D.D. Hazen sold his meat department to the McKillop brothers, but continued to operate his other businesses from this building. A.H. Phillips purchased the building in 1935.

JACKSON'S STOREFRONT, C. 1950S. Jackson's Store had a soda fountain and an early photography department. John and Blake Jackson were responsible for many photographs documenting Belchertown's history.

THE CENTER OF BELCHERTOWN, 1965. In this photo taken by Blake Jackson, Hampshire National Bank had moved into the first floor of the Masonic Building. Jackson's Store and Luncheonette, the AG Food Market, and Wallace's Hardware complete the block. In 1994, a spectacular fire destroyed this block of businesses, including Besancon's Market in the building which had once been Hazen's store. The block was rebuilt by the Vernon Lodge of Masons.

Three

Our Agricultural Legacy

Ira Shattuck. Ira Shattuck tends two Devon steers at the Eastern States Exhibition in 1930. (Courtesy of Ira Shattuck.)

The Addison Bartlett Family at Cold Spring Farm. Cold Spring Farm was located at the site of the original "cold spring," near present-day Sabin Street and Cold Spring Road. Initially, Aaron Lyman, one of the town's earliest settlers, operated an inn at this location. In 1816, the land was sold to Cyrus Bartlett. Cyrus was married to Anna Sabin, and a story relates that Cyrus and Anna were on their way from Stafford Springs, Connecticut, to Ohio when they stopped in Cold Spring to visit Anna's brother, Thomas Sabin Jr. They fell in love with the area and elected to stay. Shown here is the family of Addison Bartlett, Cyrus's son. The Bartlett farm became well known for its advanced agricultural practices, including contouring and crop rotation.

Peter Hanifin. Born in Ireland in 1860, Peter Hanifin came to America at 16. He settled first in Holyoke and then worked for 12 years on the Sabin farm. He purchased Cold Spring Farm from the Bartletts in 1902, and the Hanifin family conducted a successful fruit and dairy operation there for many years. Peter Hanifin also served two terms as town selectman. He died in 1948. (Courtesy of Agnes Hanifin.)

The Hanifin Farm. In 1961, the Fruit Growers' Association of Massachusetts purchased Cold Spring Farm from the Hanifin family and, the following year, donated 215 acres to the University of Massachusetts as a research facility. The farm is now the University of Massachusetts Horticultural Research Station on Sabin Street.

THOMAS SABIN JR. Thomas Sabin Jr. came to Belchertown from Connecticut in 1813 and purchased 100 acres. A half-century of hard work produced one of the area's premier farms. In 1871, the East Hampshire Agricultural Society awarded his farm a premium as the best managed farm in Hampshire County. At elevations over 1,000 feet, his farm and orchards afforded spectacular views. Thomas Sabin lived for 101 years, dying in 1885.

LYMAN SABIN. According to legend, every fall Thomas's son, Deacon Lyman Sabin, would hitch up his buckboard and travel 81 miles to Boston, staying at taverns and with friends. In Boston, he would sell some of his dressed hogs and purchase some needed items for the family. He would then return home leisurely, calling the whole event his "annual vacation." He died in 1897. The Sabin home burned in 1925.

Henry Jepson in the Yard of Crystal Spring Farm. Crystal Spring Farm on North Main Street was built by Dr. Estes Howe as a wedding present for his daughter Nancy when she married Ichabod Sanford in 1799. It remained a working farm into the 1950s. Henry Jepson lived across the street and operated a farm and slaughterhouse *c.* 1887.

Pansy Park, 1884. In the late nineteenth century, the Goodell family started a flower and seed business in the village of Dwight, which became widely known as "Pansy Park" after the Diamond Pansy was developed there.

Lafayette Washington Goodell. L.W. Goodell began the business in 1868 with $25 capital on his family's run-down farm. Under his management, the Goodells were shipping 50,000 orders a year worldwide by 1900. (Courtesy of Gladys Jenks.)

Lily Pond at Pansy Park. Pansy Park was famous for its rare aquatic plants and featured several ponds and pools. Among the rare aquatic plants was the Victoria Regia, a giant water lily of the Amazon with pads 4 to 5 feet across. The Goodells were the first to grow these plants outside of a greenhouse and demonstrated that they could be grown from seeds instead of from more costly plants.

The Greenhouse at Pansy Park, 1892. This photograph shows worker William Marshall in the greenhouse.

Ellen Goodell Smith and Her Son Lindsay. Dr. Ellen Goodell Smith, sister of Lafayette W. Goodell, was a doctor, author, and lecturer on healthy living. An advocate of temperance and vegetarianism, she railed against fried foods and those "who indulge in flesh that feeds and stimulates, arouses and quickens every insane desire and base passion known to mankind." Dr. Smith died from a fall at the age of 71.

Pansy Park, Dwight Station. The colorful fields at Pansy Park drew summertime travelers intent on witnessing the gorgeous floral displays of more than two thousand varieties of flowering plants, including pansies, asters, pinks, petunias, and many others. With the demise of Pansy Park, the home of Lafayette Goodell, shown here in the background, became the Pansy Park Inn. It has since been remodeled into the New Townhouse Restaurant.

Wesley M. Goodell. W.M. Goodell was born in 1846 and worked for his brother Lafayette at Pansy Park. In 1885, he became claim agent for the railroad at Dwight Station. He served the Boston & Maine and the Central Vermont Railroads for 48 years until his death. He was also postmaster at Dwight and a justice of the peace.

The Post Office, Dwight. This postcard view shows the home of Wesley M. Goodell and the Dwight Station store and post office. The post office had the only telephone in Dwight for a time. (Courtesy of Gladys Jenks.)

Arthur Howard's Petunias. The Howard family farm on Jackson Street was home to horticulturist Arthur B. Howard and his son, Everett. Among the many varieties of plants developed by A.B. Howard was the Howard Star Petunia. (Courtesy of Charles Howard.)

Howard Star Petunias. This popular strain, advertised as the "Floral Novelty of 1902," features a blossom of maroon with a white star in the center. These petunias are still grown today and can occasionally be seen in Belchertown gardens. (Courtesy of Charles Howard.)

A.B. Howard. Arthur Howard began developing his strain of petunias when he was a member of the Oneida community in Putney, Vermont. His daughter Naomi married William H. Atkins of South Amherst and they built an orcharding tradition in Atkins Farms that continues to this day. (Courtesy of Charles Howard.)

Picking Strawberries at Howard's. In the spring of 1906, Arthur Howard developed the Howard-17 strain of strawberry. It was considered "the largest and the most perfect they had ever seen." Also known as the Premier, the Howard-17 soon became popular across the North American continent. (Courtesy of Charles Howard.)

E.C. Howard, 1959. A.B. Howard died the year after the development of the Howard-17, leaving his son, Everett, to continue the business and to popularize his father's strawberries. The Howards were recognized in 1929 by the American Pomological Society with the organization's highest award, which called the Howard-17 "the most widely grown of all strawberries." Many of today's popular varieties are offsprings of Belchertown's Howard-17. (Courtesy of Charles Howard.)

Courtesy: First, Last and Always

ANY TIME

between 8 A. M. and 10 P. M. is

"Lunch Time"

Good Tea and Coffee

Ice Cream and Soda

Doughnuts, Cakes and Nut Raisin Bread

Made to Order

at

HOWARD'S HAPPY HOUR

Geraldine F. Howard, Prop.

Tel. 66

Howard's Happy Hour. In addition, the Howards operated a luncheon room and variety store on Jackson Street, which served the employees from Belchertown State School in the 1920s and 1930s. The Howards even had a small print shop where they produced their seed packets for mailing.

Sawing Wood at Shumway's Yard. These photographs depict farming scenes at the farm of E.F. Shumway on Turkey Hill.

Filling the Silo.

A Grange Exhibit at the Northampton Fair. Union Grange No. 64 was formed in 1874 as the local chapter of the National Grange, an educational, charitable, and social organization primarily for those involved in agricultural pursuits. In the 1870s, the Grange operated a cooperative store on North Main Street. This exhibit won a blue ribbon at the Northampton Fair in 1921.

Harvest Marchers of Union Grange No. 64, 1954. These dancers included Belle and Harold Peck (to the left) and Ralph Trombley (right). Pearl Very is in the background behind Belle Peck.

A Turkey Farm. Poultry was a major part of Belchertown's agriculture. Aside from numerous chicken operations, turkeys were raised on several large farms in the area, including the Anderson and Holland farms.

The Entrance to Holland Farm. In the 1930s, White Holland turkeys were sold "by means of express and parcel post" to locations all over the eastern United States. Nelson C. Holland built his poultry business from the farm on Enfield Road that had been in his family since 1803.

Belchertown Farms. Belchertown Farms was started in 1919 by Frank Fuller. With his brother, E.A. Fuller, as buyer and marketing sales manager, the farm sold milk, broilers, and eggs. In the late 1940s, the retailing of milk became predominant with the building of a pasteurizing and bottling plant. Louis Fuller, son of E.A. Fuller, carried on Belchertown Farms until 1954, when he joined the insurance firm of Bell and Hudson.

Austin Farm. This is one of the last working dairy farms in Belchertown.

Four

Education and Schools

THE LOGTOWN SCHOOL. The first record of a school in Belchertown was in 1756 when £5 was allocated to be divided among four districts comprised of 45 families, "the school to keep from nine to twelve and from one to four and the schoolmistress to ask the children twenty questions a day." Although not Belchertown's first school, the Logtown School served children of the Dwight area, or Logtown, in the early nineteenth century.

The Old Brick School, 1885. The Old Brick School in the center of town was built in 1830 by the Congregational Church for social gatherings and other events. The building was jointly used by the town and the church, serving as a school and for town meetings as well. The Old Brick School was taken down in 1888.

The Old South Center Schoolhouse. The South Center School, active from 1855 through 1900, stood on the north side of the Palmer Road less than 600 yards from the town common. It was photographed in 1934 by Edson Roderick Dorman. Eventually, Belchertown had as many as 17 school districts, most with one-room schoolhouses like this one.

The Federal Street School, 1892. Louise E. Allen was a first-year teacher in this photograph of the Federal Street School from June of 1892. The following year she moved to the Center School, where she taught for ten years.

A School Picture, 1911. Belle (Snow) Peck taught for many years at the Franklin School in South Belchertown. She is pictured here with her class from 1911.

THE ROCKRIMMON SCHOOLHOUSE. Mrs. Emma Loftus, fresh from high school in 1917, began her teaching career in the Rockrimmon Schoolhouse, shown above. The Rockrimmon School is now a private residence.

EMMA LOFTUS. Over her many years of service, Mrs. Loftus taught at several other schools in Belchertown and served as an acting principal as well. She is remembered for her tradition of holding a Thanksgiving feast for her students, tantalizing them with home-baked pies and a roast turkey, started at home, but finished at the school during the morning session. (Courtesy of Norman Loftus.)

The Union School at Dwight. The Union School replaced the Logtown School and served the Dwight area until it was closed in June of 1954, with the building of the new Cold Spring Elementary School. Emma Loftus was the last teacher at the Union School. Located on Federal Street near Route 9, the school building has been converted into a private residence. (Courtesy of Gladys Jenks.)

A School Health Pageant. Belchertown Common served as the location for this school health pageant. In 1924, the community observed Health Week with a two-day program of songs, plays, dances, and recitations by schoolchildren. Out-of-town speakers came to lecture as part of the Modern Health Crusade. One such talk was on diphtheria prevention.

Washington District School. Washington District School on Bardwell Street closed in 1939. The building is still standing and was painted red for the town's bicentennial in 1961.

Marion Shaw's Class, June 1950. Marion Shaw taught in Belchertown for 33 years, retiring in 1959. She is shown here with her fifth grade class from 1950.

Miss Orlando's Class. When Irene Orlando and her sister, Madeleine "Dotty" Lambert, retired in 1964, they had the longest tenure of any teachers in the system. Hired out of high school in 1917, Irene Orlando taught in Belchertown for 47 years. Next in seniority was her sister, who began in 1924, making an incredible 87 years of teaching experience between them. (Courtesy of Fran Loftus.)

THE BELCHERTOWN CLASSICAL SCHOOL. In 1829, Belchertown voters approved the construction of a private high school at the north end of the common. Timothy Pearl and Adolphus Strong laid the foundation, but work stopped when the proprietors had a falling out. Unfinished for six years, the Belchertown Classical School finally opened in the fall of 1835. The school's curriculum provoked controversy, however, which contributed to the school's downfall.

MARIA (FILER) STRONG. According to an account written by Mrs. Strong, her husband, Adolphus, was one of eight "public spirited men" who started the Belchertown Classical School. When the school failed to achieved financial viability, Strong offered to continue the school if the town would allow him $200 a year. When the article was passed over at town meeting, Strong was forced to discontinue the school. At first, Strong remodeled the building into tenements and later into a "temperance hotel," called the Norwattock House.

BELCHERTOWN HIGH SCHOOL, 1868. In 1867, a high school was built in the center of town as a result of a state law requiring towns with more than 500 people to have a high school. These postcards of the high school were published in 1911 to commemorate the town's 150th anniversary.

BELCHERTOWN HIGH SCHOOL, 1884.

School Picture. The classes of 1888, 1889, and 1890 are shown here with their teacher Frank J. Demond.

Belchertown High School. The high school is shown here in about 1910. Note the additions: a wing on the right side, which was used for a primary school, and the two-story addition added to the left of the main building, which served the intermediate grades. The school burned in 1921, and a year later, the Center School, an elementary school, was built on the same site.

The First B.H.S. Basketball Team. High school basketball began in Belchertown in 1903–1904. After struggling to get permission from the town to use the Old Town Hall, the boys still had to clean the hall, paint the court, and provide kerosene lamps for light. The first basketball team, from left to right, was as follows: (front row) Damon and Bridgman; (second row) Damon, Williams, Bowler (manager), and Atwood; (back row) Fairchild and Gould.

The Girls' Basketball Team. Women, too, were represented on the basketball court. This photo, taken in 1907, shows the Belchertown High School girls' basketball team. The team, from left to right, was as follows: (front row) Keyes, LaPolice, and Sanford; (back row) Alden, Bridgman, an unknown coach, Carmody, and Orlando.

A School Picture, 1923. At the time the high school burned, Lawrence Memorial Hall was being designed, stimulated by Sarah Lawrence Robinson's bequest. Town leaders were able to make additions to the design to incorporate a new regional high school. The hall itself was the center portion of the building and the wings on either side, with separate entrances, were added for the school. This picture from 1923 was photographed on the common. That year, the high school had 123 students, 25 of whom came from Enfield and Greenwich. Tom Allen, a Belchertown native, was principal of Belchertown High School from 1913 to 1936. He is seated in the front row, fifth from the left.

THE B.H.S. BASEBALL TEAM. In 1924, the Belchertown High School baseball "nine" consisted of the following, from left to right: (front row) Flaherty, Dewey, Austin, Keyes, Landers, and O'Seep; (back row) Scott, Wood, Landers, unidentified, Piper, and Belding Jackson (manager).

THE B.H.S. CLASS OF 1933. This photograph of the Class of 1933 was taken in the auditorium of Lawrence Memorial Hall.

A HIGH SCHOOL PLAY. The class play of 1953 was *The Inner Willie*, which featured, from left to right, Loretta Smith, Margot Austin, Joyce Woods, Ralph Pittsley, and Rene Daniels.

THE B.H.S. CLASS TRIP, 1967. The present high school on North Washington Street was completed in 1965. This photograph from 1967 shows high school students on a class trip to Washington, D.C. Former Senator Edward Brooke is standing in the center with then-Selectman Gerry Whitlock. Whitlock served the town in many capacities over nearly 40 years of service, including serving as the town's executive secretary for 12 years.

Five

Belchertown State School

THE BELCHERTOWN STATE SCHOOL. The Belchertown State School, a residential institution for people with mental retardation, was an important part of the community, and the town's largest employer, for over 70 years. The school officially opened in 1922 on land purchased from seven or eight families, the Town Farm, and the Deer Falls Farm.

BELCHERTOWN, MASS.,

WANTS FAMILIES AND FACTORIES

20 REASONS WHY YOU SHOULD LOCATE IN BELCHERTOWN

1. Two Railroads. 14 Passenger Trains Daily.
2. Eighty-eight miles to Boston.
3. Seventy-five miles to tide water at New London.
4. Electric Light and Power.
5. No Town Debt.
6. Low Valuation.
7. Free Factory Sites.
8. Good High and Graded Schools.
9. Several Churches.
10. $ 50,000 Free Public Library.
11. Beautiful Scenery. Three Natural Lakes.
12. Attractive "Park View" hotel - 30 Rooms.
13. New Automobile Road to Holyoke and Springfield.
14. Fertile Farming Section.
15. Ideal Summer Resort.
16. Good Social Center.
17. Beautiful Public Common.
18. Pure Air. 600 ft. above sea level.
19. No "High Cost of Living."
20. Superior Garage Facilities.

Write to THE BOARD OF TRADE, BELCHERTOWN, MASS.

A BOARD OF TRADE ADVERTISEMENT. In 1914, the Belchertown Board of Trade was established, and D.D. Hazen, "a leading merchant in town," was elected president. The mission of the board of trade was to promote Belchertown to businesses and residents from other areas seeking to relocate. The board of trade's lobbying effort in Boston was largely responsible for the state's decision to locate the school in Belchertown.

THE TOWN FARM. Originally built in 1877, the almshouse consisted of a two-story warden's house, a one-and-one-half-story ell with an indoor privy for inmates, a tramp room, and a lock-up. Inmates were wards of the town, and funds for clothing, medical treatment, etc. were administered by the selectmen. The need dwindled in the 1900s, and the building and grounds were sold to the state for the Belchertown State School.

State School Construction. Construction began in 1918 with the dormitories. Eventually, there were 13 dormitories which were home to between 50 and 150 people each. In 1961, for example, there were 1,500 residents at the school.

The Belchertown State School. The complex of buildings was like a village unto itself with its own water supply and electric plant. A farm of over 200 acres supplied milk and eggs to the Belchertown State School, the Northampton State Hospital, and the Monson State Hospital. The Belchertown State School had its own infirmary and hospital facilities, complete with operating room, dental office, pharmacy, laboratory, and X-ray department.

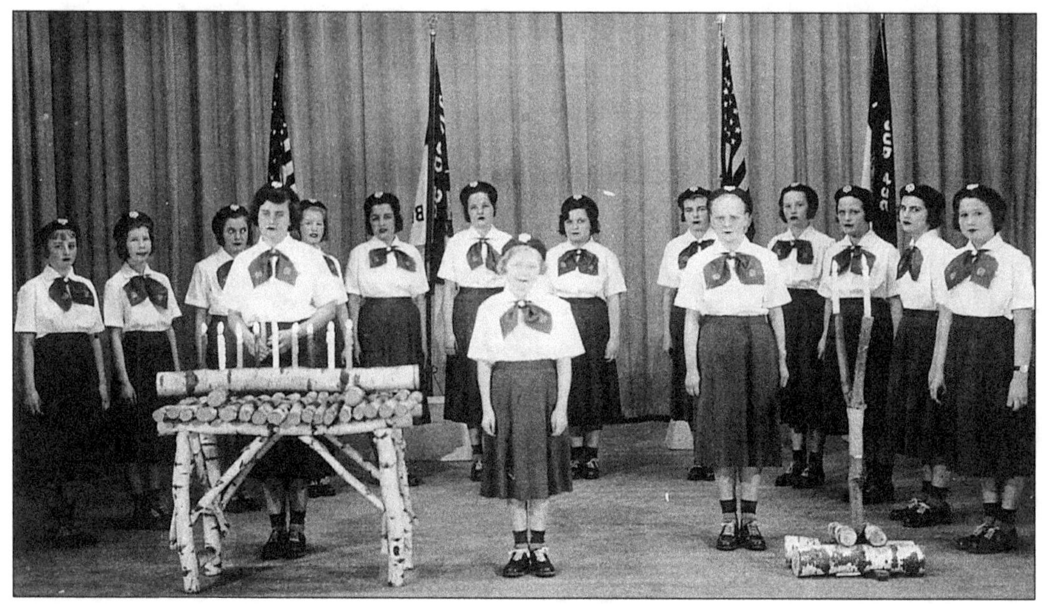

GIRL SCOUTS. The state school had its own Boy Scout and Girl Scout troops.

BOY SCOUTS.

A Belchertown State School Pageant. Residents of the state school presented many plays and pageants for the community, such as this one. Changes in the way people with mental retardation were treated resulted in de-institutionalization and the closure of Belchertown State School in the 1990s.

A Stein and Goldstein Carousel. This carousel was built about 1909 in Brooklyn. After years at Forest Lake in Palmer, it was brought to the state school in 1947 by Dr. Arthur Westwell. Its 42 horses—including 24 jumpers—all had names. Exposed to weather, the carousel deteriorated, but was restored by volunteers and returned to service in 1963. It ceased operating in 1978 and was auctioned by the state in 1993 over local objection.

TUG OF WAR. This tug of war occurred as part of the state school's Independence Day celebration in 1945.

Six

Civic Life

TOWN SEAL. Designed by Mrs. Edward Bartlett and rendered by Margot Moran for the town's bicentennial, the town seal was subsequently adopted by the town.

ELIJAH COLEMAN BRIDGMAN AND ELIZABETH J. BRIDGMAN. Elijah Coleman Bridgman (1801–1861) was one of the first American missionaries to China. He wrote the first quality translation of the Bible into the Chinese language.

WING TONG. Wing Chang Tong came to Belchertown from China to study with Mrs. Maria Longley before entering Yale College. Wing was part of the Chinese Educational Mission, a program of the Chinese government which allowed 100 boys to be educated in America. The photo is signed as follows: "To my teacher Mrs. Longley, from her good wisher and pupil, Wing C. Tong, Hartford, Ct., USA, Aug. 8th '81."

Henry Ashley Longley. Born in 1814, Henry Longley was the son of Colonel Joshua Longley, a merchant. After graduating from a seminary in Bennington, Vermont, he taught school for three years before entering his father's business in 1837. He was a major in the militia and high sheriff of Hampshire County for 25 years. He served as town clerk, treasurer, and collector for 11 years and represented Belchertown in the state legislature.

Josiah Gilbert Holland. Born in Belchertown in 1819, Dr. Josiah Gilbert Holland was a noted educator, publisher, and author. Holland became assistant editor, and later part owner, of the *Springfield Republican*. He and four others founded *Scribner's Magazine* in 1870 and he was its editor for 11 years. An author of poetry, fiction, and non-fiction works, he is known locally for his *History of Western Massachusetts*.

The Old Town Hall. The Old Town Hall on Park Street was built by Harrison Root for $2,800 in 1865 to replace an earlier structure. In 1946, extensive renovations transformed it into a gymnasium. It has always served as a recreation center for the community and the schools, with the wood-burning stoves being removed prior to basketball games. Wrestling matches were held there in the 1920s, with Dr. James Collard officiating.

A Town Meeting, 1900. Town meetings and elections were held in the Old Town Hall until 1923, when they were moved to Lawrence Memorial Hall. Elections and town meeting were held on the same day, and in this photo, the voting area can be seen against the front wall.

THE TOWN COMMON, BANDSTAND, AND SOLDIERS' MONUMENT. The Farmers and Mechanics Club built the bandstand in 1878. Erected in 1885, the Soldiers' Monument commemorates those who served in the Revolution and the Civil War. Two hundred eighty-nine men from Belchertown fought in the Civil War with 27 fatalities. A ship's mast flagpole commemorating the sinking of the battleship *Maine* during the Spanish-American War was replaced by a flagpole in 1961.

THE GRAND ARMY OF THE REPUBLIC IN FRONT OF THE GOULD BLOCK. There was a meeting room on the second floor of the Gould Block where the GAR convened. In the early 1900s, the Union Grange took over the space and met there until 1973. The Grand Army of the Republic initiated the project of building the Soldiers' Monument on the common. Funds were raised by subscription and from a town appropriation.

MYRON WALKER, DRUMMER BOY. Volunteering for the Union Army at age 14, Myron Walker became the drummer boy for Company C of the 10th Massachusetts Infantry, serving with the Army of the Potomac and frequently under fire. A story relates that Walker had once been given a silver cup and spoon by a German count impressed by Walker's rhythmic skills. Walker supposedly gave General McClellan a drink from that cup after the Battle of Fair Oaks.

THE WALKER/COLLIS HOUSE. Myron Walker was successful in the insurance business in California, and, upon his return in 1880, he had this elaborate home built on the common. The following year, Walker hosted a spectacular reunion of the 10th Massachusetts, which was attended by the governor. He served two terms in the state senate. The house was purchased by the Collis family in 1929 and was moved to Stadler Street in 1979.

Dr. Horatio Thomson. Giving new meaning to the term "family practice," two sets of father-son physicians have served Belchertown—the Thomsons and the Collards. Dr. Horatio Thomson's home and office were on South Main Street.

Dr. George Thomson. Dr. George Thomson was born in 1833. He served four years as a surgeon in the Civil War, first with the 38th Massachusetts Regiment and one year with the 26th New York Cavalry. He returned to Belchertown and practiced medicine at his father's office on South Main Street. He passed away in 1909.

Sam Stevenson with Dorothy Thomson. As a 13-year-old boy in Baltimore during the Civil War, Samuel Stevenson was hired as a servant to Adjt. Harry Walker of the First Connecticut Cavalry Regiment. Adjutant Walker was a resident of Belchertown, and when he returned after his enlistment period expired, Sam came with him. Good with horses, Sam worked as a driver and assistant to Dr. George Thomson for more than 40 years.

Margaret Stevenson with Dorothy Thomson. Sam Stevenson married Mabel Freeman, and together they raised a daughter, Margaret. Margaret Stevenson married Charles Clark, Belchertown's barber. Sam Stevenson died in 1927 at the age of 78.

A Lawn Party for the USS *Maine*. The girls in the gypsy tent told fortunes at this lawn party, probably to raise money to remove the USS *Maine* from Havana Harbor and honor those who died in the blast that began the Spanish-American War. From left to right, they are as follows: (front row) Rachel Curtis, Belle Snow, and Bertha Sanford; (back row) Annie Gibbons, Nettie Shaw, Auyella Plantiff, and Annie Fellows.

Votes for Women. Women were not able to vote in national elections until the 21st Amendment to the Constitution was passed in 1920. The suffragists in this photograph made their opinion known in Belchertown.

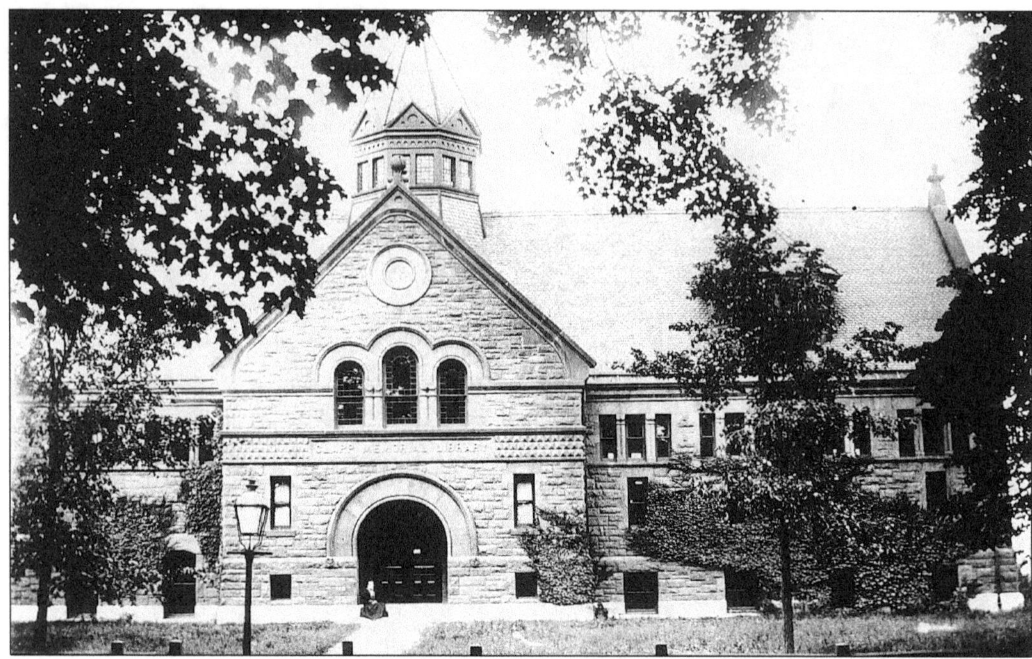

The Clapp Memorial Library. Born in Belchertown in 1818, John Francis Clapp was a successful businessman in Brooklyn, New York. Upon his death, he left a bequest of $40,000 for the construction of a library in his native town. The Clapp Memorial Library on South Main Street was dedicated on September 1, 1887. The building was designed in the shape of a Latin cross and is constructed of Longmeadow brownstone.

The Stained-Glass Window, Clapp Memorial Library. The interior of the library features two elaborate stained-glass windows with the muses of art, music, and literature as the central theme. One was given in memory of Calvin Bridgman by his wife; the other is in memory of John Francis Clapp by his brothers Everett, Edward, and Dwight.

Chauncey Walker. Corporal Walker was the first Belchertown fatality of World War I. In a letter to his mother, the company clerk wrote the following: "Chauncey was in charge of the ration detail . . . and this detail was obliged to carry them considerable distance to the woods where the company was located. It was at this time your son was hit in the arm and thigh with 'Shrapnel,' passing away at the 103rd Field Hospital." (Courtesy of American Legion Post #239.)

The Roll of Honor. Three other Belchertown soldiers died as a result of WWI. George Hannum and Warren Wright died during the war, while John Jackson succumbed later from the effects of poison gas. All four have been remembered by having streets in town named for them. In all, 70 men from Belchertown served in the Great War, and their names were placed on the Roll of Honor.

Lawrence Memorial Hall. Myron Lawrence was a prominent citizen of Belchertown who studied law with Mark Doolittle, was a member of the General Court for 27 years, and was president of the Massachusetts Senate. He brought the New London Northern Railroad through town. His daughter, Sarah, married Dr. Charles Robinson, a Belchertown doctor who moved west and became active in the Free Soil movement in "bleeding Kansas" before the Civil War. He later was elected governor of the territory of Kansas. When Sarah died suddenly in 1911, she bequeathed money for the construction of Lawrence Memorial Hall in her parents' honor. The building was erected in 1923.

The Stone House Museum. Jonathan Dwight built the Stone House as a gift to his daughter Diantha when she married Theodore Dwight Lyman in 1827. After many years in the Dwight family, this spacious house was purchased from heirs in 1922 for the use of the Belchertown Historical Association. This Federal style home contains superb examples of American furniture, china, and decorative accessories made in the eighteenth and nineteenth centuries.

The Ford Annex. Henry Ford donated money for the construction of the Ford Annex. Ford's interest in the town stemmed from his friendship and business relationship with Belchertown native Gaston Plantiff. The stone work was done by local stonemasons D.P. Spencer and his son, Howard. The building, dedicated in 1923, houses a collection of carriages made in Belchertown.

THE PARK ASSOCIATION RAKING THE COMMON, 1935. The Belchertown Park Association first formed in 1873, reorganized in 1893, and was incorporated in 1904 with the Village Improvement Society. In the year of its formation, the Town granted the association certain rights and privileges regarding the common to protect it from "mutilation and nuisance." These privileges included the right to fence it and adorn it "with shade and ornamental trees."

WANTED:

100 MEN

with iron rakes

for one hour

Let's Surprise Your Old Common

and ourselves too

Thurs., April 19, at 8 a. m.

Park Assn. Clean-up Committee

H. F. Peck
J. J. Kempkes
H. R. Gould
M. C. Baggs
E. C. Howard

AN ADVERTISEMENT FOR VOLUNTEERS. Dependent on volunteer labor, the Park Association used the Patriot's Day holiday for spring cleaning on the common. The association was permitted to keep any income derived from cutting the grass.

The Engine House, Belchertown Fire Department. The Enterprise Hook and Ladder Company was organized in 1887 by local businessmen. After a conflagration in 1899, the town formed a fire department, appropriating $900 for apparatus and $500 for a building. Completed in 1902, the fire station has served for nearly a century. In 1998, a new fire station is being constructed on the adjacent lot where Loman Smith's house stands in this view.

The Fire Department, 1932. In December of 1899, members of the Enterprise Hook and Ladder Company signed up to become the Belchertown Fire Department. The Belchertown Firefighters' Association was formed in 1929.

WALTER AND LEWIS BLACKMER (LEFT). The *Belchertown Sentinel* published its first issue on April 2, 1915, with over 200 subscribers paying 5¢ per copy. Its founder, editor, and publisher for 50 years was Lewis Blackmer, shown here with his brother Walter, who often assisted in the publication. The *Sentinel* was printed in a shop on the Blackmer's Cottage Street property. The old printing press and other equipment can now be seen in the Blackmer Print Shop at the Stone House Museum.

LEWIS BLACKMER AND PETER DEARNESS. When Lewis Blackmer retired from the *Sentinel* in 1965, he turned over the reins to his apprentice and assistant, Peter Dearness. Dearness modernized the paper and expanded coverage to include Granby. The paper was sold in 1973 to Turley Publications, the paper's current publishers.

Dr. James Collard. Dr. James Collard (1881–1962) was a widely respected physician who practiced medicine in Belchertown and the surrounding communities into his eighties. He was school physician for over 50 years and was active in the Masons, the Lions Club, the Congregational Church, the Fireman's Association, and served his community in many other ways. Dr. Collard's home and office were on Maple Street, but he was a true country doctor, traveling by horse and buggy in the early days to visit his patients. (Courtesy of Rachel Collard.)

Dr. Kenneth Collard. In 1949, Dr. Ken Collard began his medical practice in Belchertown after serving in the U.S. Army. His first office was on the common. He practiced in Belchertown for 34 years, retiring in 1983. He was also the school physician. (Courtesy of Rachel Collard.)

Swift River Valley. In order to provide water for the Boston metropolitan area, the Swift River was dammed to create the Quabbin Reservoir, submerging the towns of Dana, Prescott, Enfield, and Greenwich. Many of the residents of these towns, and some of their homes, were relocated to Belchertown. These postcards show the reservoir as it filled over a seven-year period.

Quabbin Reservoir as Seen from the Dike.

CONSTRUCTION AT QUABBIN. Construction of the Windsor Dam and the Goodnough Dike lasted from 1933 through 1939. In order to transport the water, a long aqueduct pipeline was laid between the Quabbin and Wachusett Reservoirs and then farther east to supply many Massachusetts communities.

THE QUABBIN SPILLWAY. In addition to its value as a drinking water source, the Quabbin Reservoir is one of the finest recreational areas in western Massachusetts. Its miles of beautiful hiking trails and picnic areas are popular with local residents and visitors alike. Limited boat fishing and deer hunting are possible in season.

GIRL SCOUTS, VETERANS' WELCOME HOME PARADE, 1946. On July 4, 1946, a large celebration was held in Belchertown to welcome the returning veterans from the Second World War. These photographs show the parade in the center of town and at the Belchertown State School.

THE VETERANS' WELCOME HOME PARADE, 1946. This is American Legion Post #239, named in honor of Corporal Chauncey D. Walker.

SOME SUNDAY MORNING, WELCOME HOME PARADE, 1946. These floats depicted an image of the life to which the veterans were returning.

THE 1946 WELCOME HOME PARADE.

The Bicentennial Parade, Belchertown Historical Association. In 1961, the town celebrated the bicentennial of its incorporation. In this Blake Jackson photo, Mrs. Richard Pratt, Gerald G. Tremaine, Mrs. Elliott Cordner, and George Poole ride in the stagecoach of the Belchertown Historical Association. Kenneth Henneman rides atop the coach.

The Bicentennial Parade, Bushy Boys. During the town's bicentennial celebration, some of the men grew elaborate facial hair and were dubbed the "Bushy Boys." A contest was held and prizes were given. Shown here are Edmund Wallace (left), of Wallace's Hardware, and William Squires, who served several terms as a Belchertown selectman.

The Bicentennial Parade, Belchertown Fire Department. The Belchertown Fire Department's entry in the Bicentennial Parade included the antique pumper known as the Mary Jane. Elwyn Bock, Raymond Menard, and Harry Brougham are shown from left to right in this Blake Jackson photo.

The Bicentennial Town Crier. J. Raymond Gould served as town crier for the bicentennial celebration. He was proprietor of the Esso gasoline station in the center of town, now the R & W Service Station.

The Bicentennial, Dedication of War Memorial. Veterans of the two World Wars and the Korean Conflict are remembered on bronze plaques near the flagpole on the common. The flagpole was erected in 1961, replacing the ship's mast honoring the Spanish-American War veterans. Two Belchertown men died in action in the Vietnam conflict, Michael P. Austin and Roger C. Gaughan, for whom Austin-Gaughan Field is named.

Seven

Religion and the Churches

The Congregational Church. The Congregational meetinghouse was dedicated on September 12, 1792. This building has been remodeled several times over the years. Originally, the structure was nearly square with an entryway from the west, or facing the common. The high pulpit was on the east wall and there were galleries on three sides. Major remodeling occurred in 1872, when the galleries were removed, the interior re-arranged, and the large windows constructed.

REV. LYMAN COLEMAN. Rev. Lyman Coleman served Belchertown from 1825 until 1832. In addition to his ecclesiastical accomplishments, he was an educator of merit, having taught grammar school in Hartford, English at Phillips Academy in Andover, German at Princeton College, and ancient languages at Lafayette College in Pennsylvania. Reverend Coleman also taught in Amherst and was principal of Burr Seminary in Vermont. He authored books on sacred geography and other subjects connected to Christian antiquities.

THE PRISCILLAS, 1917. The Priscillas were a social group that raised monies for various charities during the First World War.

THE HOME DEPARTMENT, 1949. The Congregational Church has had a number of women's groups through the years. Suppers, bazaars, and other kinds of fund-raising activities were conducted for the church's needs and other local causes. The Home Department is still active today.

THE CONGREGATIONAL CHURCH PARISH HOUSE. The Congregational Church Parish House sits next door to the church and is used for Sunday school classes, meetings, and social functions. It was built in 1888 on the site of the Old Brick School and has been enlarged several times since.

THE SUNDAY SCHOOL IN THE NEW ADDITION. Sunday school was taught in the new addition to the Parish House. Shown here in about 1954 is Doris Dickinson working with a diligent class of students. The children are, from left to right, Loren Shumway, Richard Juskalian, Linda Henneman, Judy Dickinson, Sue Skinner, Donna Fleurent, John Plowucha, and Karl Berger.

THE ST. FRANCIS CHURCH. This building was originally for the Brainerd Church, a second Congregational group formed as a result of dissension over the Masonic order. When these churches reunited, the building became a Baptist church until that society disbanded in 1913. The building then served as a Community Hall during which time its steeple was removed. It was acquired in 1923 by the Catholic Church, and the first resident pastor was Rev. James Dunphy in 1925.

FR. GEORGE R. DUDLEY. Father Dudley arrived from Monson to become pastor at Belchertown in December of 1951 and remained until his death in 1969 at the age of 68. From the beginning, the parish in Belchertown conducted services at the Belchertown State School.

St. Adalbert's Church. Originally, Polish immigrants to Bondsville and South Belchertown were members of St. Bartholomew's parish. In 1902, Bondsville became a mission of Sts. Peter and Paul Church in Three Rivers. In 1913, Father Kulpa initiated the design and construction of St. Adalbert's Church, completed under the direction of Father Krzywda. The cornerstone was laid in 1916 and the church was blessed in June 1918. The rectory behind the church was originally intended as a parochial school.

The Methodist Church. By 1819, there was a Methodist meetinghouse in South Belchertown, but demand continued for services in the town center. The Methodist Episcopal Church was organized by Theodore Blodgett and Thomas Haskell in 1865. The first pastor, Reverend William Gordon, held services at both locations, traveling from South Belchertown to minister in the Old Town Hall. In 1873, the Methodist Society purchased the Union Street Church, the oldest Methodist church in Springfield, and rebuilt it in Belchertown center.

Enfield Sunday at the Methodist Church. The Methodist Episcopal Church in Enfield, Massachusetts, officially dissolved in May 1934, with the creation of the Quabbin Reservoir. A memorial tablet was placed in the church and for many years Enfield Sunday was observed in Belchertown.

Reverend and Mrs. Smith. Rev. Rockwell C. Smith, known as "Rocky," was pastor of the Methodist church from 1928 to 1937. He and his wife, Frances, wrote several plays that were presented in the church in the 1930s. Out of this endeavor came a community theater group called the "Belchertown Players," who produced many successful plays in Lawrence Memorial Hall.

Dwight Chapel. The cornerstone of Dwight Chapel, a non-sectarian church located on Federal Street, was laid in October 1886, and the building was dedicated on March 12, 1887. The chapel was built on land donated by Mrs. Elizabeth R. Wilson and Patrick Joy and was named in honor of Harrison Dunbar Dwight, the first freight agent for Dwight Station. Funds for the chapel were raised through a variety of creative endeavors.

Dwight Chapel, 1887. Mrs. Austin Dickinson of Amherst pledged the first $200, and she and Mrs. Robert Harmon raised the money by making and selling 1,500 pot holders. Another group made a quilt, placing the autographs of President Cleveland, his First Lady, and his mother in the center and then charged neighbors 10¢ to embroider their own names into it. Others sold jellies, teas, aprons, and other products.

Eight

Recreation and Entertainment

THE ARRIVAL OF THE SPECIAL TRAIN ON CATTLE SHOW DAY. The Belchertown Fair is one of the oldest, continuously held fairs in New England.

THE BELCHERTOWN CATTLE SHOW. The Belchertown Fair has been a special day in town since the first one was held in 1856. Originally called the Belchertown Cattle Show, it was for many years sponsored by the Farmers and Mechanics Club, which was known as the Belchertown Agricultural and Mechanics Association until 1860. This view is from a postcard and was taken about 1911.

THE BELCHERTOWN FAIR, HORSES AND CATTLE. Early cattle shows were considered rather rowdy affairs, with swindling games, bawdy entertainment, and sideshows. Alcoholic beverages were sold in town, and in 1887, a buggy of the Weston family was capsized by the antics of a drunken driver, occasioning a bitter look at the number of "groggeries" in town.

The Fair Day Parade. The parade on Fair Day gave everyone a chance to show off their produce, livestock, crafts, and wares. In the early days, so many oxen were in the parade that they could completely encircle the common. Fifty-three yokes of cattle were in the 1887 parade, which also included a barber shop on wheels.

Belchertown's Fair. This photo shows D.F. Shumway and a bevy of young ladies on a float.

Dr. Francis M. Austin. The town's well-known veterinarian, Dr. Austin is remembered by townspeople as the longtime marshal of the Belchertown Fair Parade, which he led on his mounts Kentucky and Lady Denmark. An expert horseman, Dr. Austin competed in major East Coast shows. In his practice, he pioneered the use of oxygen and antibiotic therapy in animals. He also served as selectman for 29 years. (Courtesy of Margot Moran.)

The Elm Farm Float, Fair Day Parade. Recently, as the number of working farms has diminished, the Belchertown Fair has become an "old home day" for the town. Put on by volunteers and the Friends of the Fair, the fair is privately funded, using no town money. In addition to rides, games, and entertainment, the fair still includes ox and horse pulls and other agricultural competitions as a reminder of our heritage.

Ida Plantiff King on Bicycle. Ida Plantiff King was the sister of Gaston Plantiff, regional sales manager for the Ford Motor Company and a personal friend of Henry Ford. Here, Ida tests out a different mode of transportation and recreation. Gaston was a bicyclist, as well, and possessed many racing trophies.

Belchertown Residents in Cars. A group of prominent Belchertown men gathered on Sundays at D.F. Shumway's farm to work on their automobiles and go for excursions. Among those in this photo are Fred Walker, Edward Schmidt, Roy Shaw, Ed Fuller, Harry Hopkins, John Jackson, Guy Allen Sr., George Jackson, William Orlando, Rudd Fairchild, A.W. Stacey, Harry Ward, and Milton Baggs. Dr. James Collard is second from the left, wearing the bowler.

CAMPING ON THE SWIFT RIVER. Around the turn of the century, a group of Belchertown men set up camp on the Swift River. This photo shows Fred Purdy (left) and Herb Shaw with all the comforts of home.

DYER'S POND AND PARK ISLAND. Dyer's Pond, also known as Dorman's Pond, was at the end of Jensen Road off Jabish Street. L.W. Dillon, a Belchertown businessman, built a small dance pavilion and several summer cottages on an island in the pond, which he called Park Island. With Japanese lanterns and soft music, Park Island was a romantic retreat for visitors at the Park View Hotel and for local residents, too.

Skating on the Common. The town common provided a suitable skating rink on frosty winter afternoons.

A Variety Show. Variety shows and minstrel shows have long been a part of Belchertown's entertainment. Here is one such show performed at the Methodist church as part of a Lion's Club function. From left to right, the performers are Claude Smith, Larry Graham, Ken Collard, and Carl Peterson.

Holland Glen. Named for Josiah G. Holland, the glen is a "deep, narrow chasm with steep sides covered thickly with a growth of pine and hemlock." The water through the glen "spreads off a vast ledge, falling about 25 feet . . . then goes tumbling over the rocks, descending about 200 feet in a distance of half a mile . . ." A favorite spot for hikers, Holland Glen is owned by the Belchertown Historical Association.

Lake Metacomet. Belchertown has three lovely lakes, once known as Upper, Middle, and Lower Ponds, or the Bridgman Ponds. John Jackson proposed the names by which they are known today: Lake Holland, Lake Arcadia, and Lake Metacomet. Simon Kelley gave the town land on Lake Arcadia that is now the Town Beach. This photo shows two members of the Belchertown Camera Club at Lake Metacomet.

Nine

Around the Town: Scenes and People

DEVON LANE FARM. For years, the Devon Lane Farm was known for its Great Danes. The dog with the pail was trained to take the feed out to the chickens. (Courtesy of Ira Shattuck.)

Timothy Kenfield and Joshua Sibley. These two Belchertown men share a ride in a one-horse chaise. Supposedly, the chaise was once owned by Dr. Estes Howe, the town's first physician. Kenfield was known for his talent on the fiddle.

Henry Bracey. Henry Bracey lived on Munsell Street in Belchertown for 60 years, having come from Waterbury, Connecticut, with his parents, George and Sarah Bracey. He was an employee of the Central Vermont Railroad for many years before working for the Metropolitan District Commission at Quabbin Park Cemetery. He died in 1969 at the age of 75. Henry is remembered for his sense of humor and his hand-rolled cigarettes.

Eddie Parent, the Popcorn Man. His newspaper advertisement read as follows: "This is to announce that I have opened a hot popcorn stand in front of Clark's Barber Shop and shall be happy to serve you. I use Conkey's popcorn—home grown." Eddie Parent was a WWI veteran and member of the "40 and 8," a veterans' organization named for the number of soldiers and mules that could fit in a French boxcar.

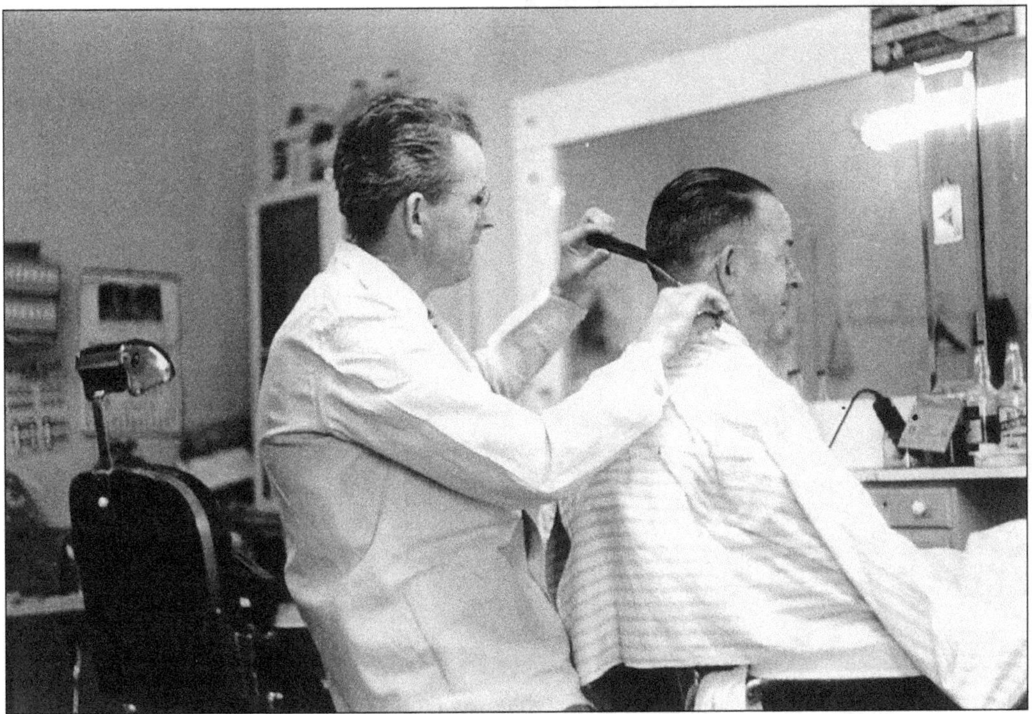

Johnny the Barber. Johnny Midura came from Bondsville in the 1930s to barber in Belchertown center. Bill Webster is in the chair.

South Main Street, Hurricane of 1938. In September of 1938, a ferocious hurricane hit the East Coast and New England without warning. Homes and businesses suffered damages and Belchertown lost many of the ancient elms that lined its streets. This is South Main Street in an Edwin Schmidt photograph.

Downing's Hen House. Many of the poultry farms were decimated by the hurricane. Edward Downing's hen house was on Federal Street. One poultry man reported that his chickens came wandering home for days after the storm.

Elisha Warner. This Elisha Warner, one of Belchertown's legendary characters, was the foster son of Capt. Elisha Warner, whose name he took. It is said that Lisha was superstitious about having his picture taken, but entered a traveling photographer's cart for this photo for a bribe of 25¢. When he died, a resident of the town farm, he was granted his oft-spoken wish—to be buried in a silver-handled coffin.

Fernando Shaw, Rural Free Delivery. Perhaps the first RFD service in Belchertown was provided by Fernando Shaw. Born in Belchertown in 1841, he served in the Civil War. One early account states that he used a pair of horses to pull a sizable carriage in better weather. He died in 1925 at the age of 84.

OLD MEN OF BELCHERTOWN. John W. Jackson, an early photography enthusiast and historian, documented much of the town's history with his camera. Sometime between 1905 and 1910, he shot a series of glass-plate negatives depicting the "Old Men of Belchertown," some of which are reproduced on this page and the next. The subject of this photo is unknown.

ALONZO RANDALL. Mr. Randall died in 1916 at the age of 92.

James Harvey Davis. When James H. Davis died in 1911 at the age of 93, he was the oldest man in town and still active. Formerly a carpenter, a cabinetmaker, and a blacksmith, he picked huckleberries and made canes in his retirement. He was a lifelong resident of Belchertown and his house still stands at 39 North Main Street.

Merrick Whittemore. A 1914 newspaper article stated, "It would be quite difficult to find a man who bears a closer resemblance to the mythical Father Time than does Merrick Whittemore of this town. When he is in the hayfield, all that is necessary to complete the picture is a flowing garb and the symbolic hour glass. Although he is 73 years of age, he is extremely active and is a familiar character."

CONTENTMENT IN BELCHERTOWN. This Clifton Johnson photograph says it all. (Courtesy of Jones Library, Amherst.)

www.ingramcontent.com/pod-product-compliance
Lightning Source LLC
LaVergne TN
LVHW081530100826
845153LV00004B/243

* 9 7 8 1 5 3 1 6 6 0 2 0 8 *